My Name : ....

My Age   : ....

This a little book is !

FOR
YOU

Enjoy every moment
while reading it

Hello
Memorial Day!

Memorial Day is a time for remembering. It honors U.S. soldiers who fought and died for our country's freedom.

Memorial day is an the last Monday of May.It is a national holiday.Governement offices and schools are closed that day.

On Memorial Day,U.S flogs fly at half_stalf.Lowering them shows respect people,also put flowers and flags on soldier's groves.

How it Began

Americans first celebrated Memorial Day in the 1800s. They called it Decoration Day. It honored soldier's who had died in the Civil war (1861_1865).

The name changed
to Memorial Day in 1882
The holiday soon became
day to honor U.S.Soldiers
from all wars.

Memorial Day is a sad day
But it's also a happy day
Americans celebrate freedom
and give thenks for living
in a free Country.

*Let's
celebrated*

It's Memorial Day !
How will you celebrate?
spend time with your family
and friends.Heve a picnic,
play sports or go to the the beach.

Honor Soldiers by flying
a U.S. flag write letters
to Soldiers serving to day.
Thank them by shoring
a picture you drew.

Many cities have parades
On memorial Day.
Listen to marching bands.
Remember the soldiers
who fought to keep us free.

Finally
Love you selfL
Love your Parents
Love you Country

Thank you

for getting to this point

Made in United States
Orlando, FL
23 July 2022

20068754R00015